*Israel Bernbaum, **Remember!!**, 1983, oil on canvas, 20 x 40-¼ in.*

Israel Bernbaum
Painting His Story
In Commemoration of the 70th Year Anniversary of the Warsaw Ghetto Uprising

MONTCLAIR STATE UNIVERSITY

GEORGE SEGAL GALLERY
montclair.edu/segalgallery

1 Normal Ave., Montclair, NJ 07043

(973) 655-3382; Fax (973) 655-7665

February 26–April 21, 2013

Dr. Batya Brutin, Guest Curator

*Israel Bernbaum, **Untitled**, 1981, oil on canvas, 36 x 24-¼ in.*

Contents

5	Message from President Susan A. Cole
6	Message from Mark S. Levenson, Past President, Jewish Federation of Greater Clifton-Passaic, New Jersey
8	Message from Dean Daniel Gurskis, College of the Arts
9	Message from Valerie Sharfman, Director Emeritus, Holocaust Resource Center of Greater Clifton-Passaic, New Jersey
11	Foreword and Acknowledgments from Director M. Teresa Lapid Rodriguez, George Segal Gallery
12	Dr. Batya Brutin, In Commemoration of the 70th Year Anniversary of the Warsaw Ghetto Uprising in 1943
29	Exhibition Plates
54	Exhibition Checklist
55	Sponsors
56	Program Presenters & Lender

*Israel Bernbaum, **Untitled**, from studies for **On Both Sides of the Warsaw Ghetto Wall**, n.d. pencil on paper, 11-7/8 x 13-15/16 in.*

A Message from President Susan A. Cole

In 1943, Jewish resistance arose in Warsaw in German-occupied Poland to oppose the Nazi effort to transport the remaining Ghetto population to the Treblinka extermination camp. Although it was eventually crushed, the Warsaw Ghetto Uprising constituted the largest single revolt by Jews against Nazism during the Second World War. Montclair State University's George Segal Gallery commemorates the 70th anniversary of the Warsaw Ghetto Uprising with an exhibition of murals and drawings by Israel Bernbaum.

Bernbaum was born in Warsaw but fled the city at the age of 18 when Hitler invaded Poland. Eventually making his way to New York City, Bernbaum pursued an artistic career with the clear goal of documenting the Warsaw Ghetto and the Holocaust. In 2011, a collection of his work entered the Montclair State art collection as a generous gift from the Holocaust Resource Center of the Jewish Federation of Greater Clifton-Passaic. Dr. Batya Brutin, the director of Holocaust Studies and the Israeli Society Program at Beit Berl Academic College in Israel, has served as curator of the exhibition.

I invite you not only to tour the exhibition — and to bring your children, for whom Bernbaum created much of his art — but also to take advantage of the lectures, workshops, and concert that will accompany it.

A Message from Mark S. Levenson, Past President
The Jewish Federation of Greater Clifton-Passaic, New Jersey

*Israel Bernbaum, three untitled studies for **On Both Sides of the Warsaw Ghetto Wall,** n.d. pencil on paper. From top to bottom, 15-15/16 x 12 in., 4-9/16 x 9-1/4 in., 17-7/8 x 11-7/8 in.*

The *Holocaust,* also known as the *Shoah* (catastrophe), was the systematic mass murder of approximately six million Jews during World War II by Adolf Hitler, Nazi Germany, and collaborating countries and regimes throughout Europe. The genocide of six million Jews—over one and a half million of whom were children—wiped out two thirds of European Jewry and one third of world Jewry. The Holocaust was unique in its evil, its design, and its targeting of the Jewish people. The mass use of gas chambers and crematoria, concentration and slave labor camps, death marches, mass shootings, starvation, medical experimentation, sterilizations, increasingly shrinking Jewish "ghettos," and inhumanely packed freight train transports to extermination camps—all in the wide open and with the complicity of supposedly civilized people—was heretofore unknown in the annals of history. Every arm of German bureaucracy (and similar government involvement by their collaborating states) was involved in the worst perpetration of evil in the 20th century, if not all of history.

No Jew was immune to or exempt from the Nazi reach. Nobel laureates, German-Jewish military heroes, artisans, craftsman, athletes, intellectuals, scholars, educators, medical professionals, politicians and civil service government employees, lawyers, bankers, businessmen and -women, students, housewives, children and babies, secular Jews and unaffiliated Jews as well as observant Jews, were all targeted, trapped, crushed, and destroyed.

Out of the ashes of the Holocaust, the remnants of European Jewry mainly found refuge in two countries—the modern state of Israel and the United States of America. While entry into either of the two future home countries of the ragged Holocaust survivors was by no means easy or assured, Israel and the United States proved to be the major welcoming and integrating centers for the survivors. Many survivors flourished and thrived here in the United States and became patriotic citizens of a great country that provided a safe, secure, and relatively discrimination-free home that had not been known or enjoyed by the Jews of the Diaspora in many centuries, if ever.

The survivors became, in many instances, both literally and figuratively, the builders of new homes in their communities, and of their broader communities, and became active and involved contributing and charitable citizens and patriots. In our local area of Passaic-Clifton, as in many other cities and towns in New Jersey and the United States, the survivors not only gave back to the communities and those in need, but also began to create and build institutions that would memorialize the Holocaust and teach about the sad history, so as to educate current and future generations in order to help prevent any such future evil from being perpetrated ever again.

One of the primary and outstanding examples of such research and teaching institutions was the Holocaust Resource Center in Greater Clifton-Passaic, founded and built by a beloved Holocaust survivor Joseph Bukiet and his family. The award-winning Holocaust Resource Center was housed for its entire existence in the Jewish Community Center (YM-YWHA) building at 199 Scoles Avenue in Clifton and was also brilliantly and capably led by noted Holocaust educator Valerie Sharfman. The Holocaust Resource Center provided quality programming, Holocaust education and guidance, and support to survivors.

With the recent sale of the Jewish Community Center building in Clifton, the need to find a new, permanent home for portions of the Holocaust Resource Center's collections became apparent. After consideration of many locations, the committee charged with finding a new home for the collections unanimously and enthusiastically approved the transfer of its art and library to Montclair State University. The Jewish Federation of Greater Clifton Passaic and the Holocaust Resource Center are proud of our partnership with Montclair State and strongly believe we have made the right choice for the permanent new home of our Holocaust art and library collection.

A Message from Dean Daniel Gurskis
College of the Arts

Israel Bernbaum, **Untitled,** *from studies for* **On Both Sides o fthe Warsaw Ghetto Wall,** *n.d. graphite on paper, 10-15/16 x 14-1/16 in.*

As recent events both in this country and abroad remind us, inhumanity is an ever-present risk of the human condition. Sadly, the victims are most often those least able to defend themselves—children. At no time has inhumanity been more savage or more chilling than during the Holocaust: more than six million people murdered, over one and a half million of them children.

The German statesman Richard von Weizsäcker observed, "Whoever refuses to remember the inhumanity is prone to new risks of infection." The work of Israel Bernbaum, in its meticulous documentation of the destruction of the Warsaw Ghetto, does not ask us to remember; it compels us to. And it often directs its most powerful messages to the younger generation, those best equipped to fashion a future that does not repeat the past.

This exhibit, **Israel Bernbaum Paints His Story**, is timed to commemorate the seventieth anniversary of the Warsaw Ghetto Uprising, the largest single act of Jewish resistance during World War II. We are pleased that you have come to the Segal Gallery and that we are able to share this important work with you.

A Message from Valerie Sharfman, Director Emeritus
Holocaust Resource Center of Jewish Federation of Greater Clifton-Passaic, New Jersey

Detail from **Jewish Children in Warsaw Ghetto and in Death Camps,** 1981, oil on canvas, 70-3/8 x82-1/4 in.

When I first met Israel Bernbaum at an educators' conference, he showed me his book, **My Brother's Keeper: The Holocaust through the Eyes of an Artist** (G.P. Putnam & Sons, 1985), and he requested my help in getting it republished. I was immediately struck by the power of his images. After his death in 1993, his art and written materials were bequeathed to the Holocaust Resource Center "to be used for Holocaust education of children and to teach love for and tolerance of people of all faiths, nationalities, and races." Although we were a small facility, we did our best to fulfill his wishes.

I am gratified that with this exhibit by the George Segal Gallery Israel Bernbaum's art and message will reach a much wider and more diverse audience.

Israel Bernbaum, **Untitled:** *complete study for* **The Warsaw Ghetto Uprising—Heroism and Resistance,** *n.d., graphite on paper*

Foreword and Acknowledgments
M. Teresa Lapid Rodriguez, Director
George Segal Gallery

This exhibition commemorates the 70th anniversary of the Warsaw Ghetto Uprising through presentation of Israel Bernbaum's murals and drawings. Done in the 1980s, the six murals and hundreds of drawings entered the permanent collection of Montclair State University in 2011 as generous gifts from the Jewish Federation of Greater Clifton-Passaic and the Holocaust Resource Center of Clifton, New Jersey. The works served as illustrations for his award-winning book, **My Brother's Keeper: The Holocaust through the Eyes of an Artist**. Rendered in childlike manner, the works had in mind the over one and a half million children lost to the Holocaust to whom the book is dedicated. Bernbaum had one goal in mind—that children are to remember that they are their brothers' keepers.

A second goal for the Segal Gallery's exhibition is the examination of the aesthetic merit of the works and recognition of Israel Bernbaum as an artist. Because of the subject matter, the curator must be thoroughly knowledgeable about the Holocaust and its aesthetics to deliver a proper interpretation of works in context. And, with the help of former Holocaust Resource Center director Ms. Valerie Sharfman, the curator was identified— Dr. Batya Brutin, director of Holocaust Studies and the Israeli Society Program at Beit Berl Academic College, Israel.

The exhibition pieces are not without challenges, as their condition ranges from good to poor. Many of the drawings in particular, at times bone chilling in their depiction of the subject matter, can not be shown until they are restored to an exhibitable state. We hope to attract support for restoration of these valuable works.

I have many individuals and organizations to thank for this wonderful exhibition: Curator Dr. Batya Brutin, who has done a great job laying out the works, writing an essay for the catalog, and providing lectures on the aesthetics of the Bernbaum murals as well as on the wider issue of the aesthetics of Holocaust Art; Inge Auerbacher, Holocaust survivor and author of **I am a Star: Child of the Holocaust,** to speak about her personal experience in Terezin; Erika Bleiberg, writer and publicist; Gail Tarkan Shube, graphic designer; Jose Camacho of Midland Gallery; Tena Mancini of Artist Frame Gallery; Susan Werk, education director of Congregation Agudath Israel; Teddi Dolph and the Segal Gallery board; and the dedicated Segal Gallery staff have all worked hard to support this exhibition and help it find a major audience in the region.

We are pleased to have the Jewish Federation and former Holocaust Resource Center of Greater Clifton-Passaic, New Jersey and the Holocaust Council of Greater Metro West, Jewish Federation of Greater Metro West as enthusiastic endorsers of the event. In full support from Montclair State are President Susan A. Cole, Provost Willard Gingerich, Vice President John Shannon, and College of the Arts Dean Daniel Gurskis. The exhibition is also rich in collaborations from the College of the Arts, College of Humanities and Social Sciences, Harry N. Sprague Library, Global Education Center, the Jewish American Studies Program, and Cali School of Music. Funds from the New Jersey State Council on The Arts, The John McMullen Family Foundation, and proceeds from the Segal Gallery annual fundraiser, **Art Connections 8,** made the exhibition possible.

Israel Bernbaum
Painting His Story
In Commemoration of the 70th Year Anniversary of the Warsaw Ghetto Uprising
by Dr. Batya Brutin

Introduction

Israel Bernbaum, a Holocaust survivor and artist, painted "His Story" with detailed visual portrayals of both his own personal story as well as the plight of the Warsaw Jews during the Holocaust. Bernbaum's work is the manifestation of his promise to himself to disseminate the story of the Holocaust. He wrote:

Lines, shapes and color are my language. . . I want to talk through my paintings to all the people of the world. The story of the Holocaust must be of concern to everyone.[1] *My paintings are only a modest contribution to the moral obligation of telling about the Holocaust.*[2]

Bernbaum was born in Warsaw, Poland, in 1911. Before World War II, Warsaw was the largest and most vital cultural Jewish community, not only in Poland, but in all of Europe. Bernbaum experienced the Nazi invasion of Poland on September 1, 1939, although he and his family escaped shortly after by crossing the border into the Soviet Union. On October 12, 1940, on Yom Kippur (The Day of Atonement), the Nazis decreed the creation of a Jewish ghetto in Warsaw and established the segregated area within a few days. Out of 1,800 streets in the city, only 73 were included in the ghetto. The Jewish population was ordered to finance and erect a three-meter-high wall around these streets. On November 16, 1940, the ghetto was closed, and the residents were locked inside.[3]

Upon arriving in the Soviet Union, Bernbaum was separated from his parents and brother and never saw them again. Since he was eighteen years old at the time, he was shipped to Siberia and recruited—against his will—into the Soviet Army. After the war, all former Polish citizens, including Bernbaum, were sent back to Poland. The emptiness, destruction, and the anti-Semitic atmosphere he found in his birthplace horrified him, and Bernbaum left Poland for Paris, where he stayed for ten years before immigrating to the United States. In the U.S., he built a new life for himself, studied art at Queens College, and graduated in 1973. Bernbaum's final college project, ***On Both Sides of the Warsaw Ghetto Wall***, was the first work he produced about the Holocaust. The subject was, as he said, in his mind and heart,[4] and he continued to create Holocaust-inspired art from that point on. When he died in 1993, Israel Bernbaum left the world the precious inheritance of his artwork.

Bernbaum aimed his art mostly at a young audience, using a naïve, almost cartoon-like style. He chose topics, images and colors that

*Israel Bernbaum, **Untitled: complete study for On Both Sides of the Warsaw Ghetto Wall,** 1972, graphite on paper, 40-¾ x 58-½ in.*

Warsaw Ghetto

presented the horrible fate of the Jewish people during the Holocaust in a format that young people could understand and cope with. He wrote: "I, however, have tried to revive the Holocaust in my large paintings—in bold, sharp colors, heavy lines, and through various arrangements of figures and shapes."[5]

Since Bernbaum did not experience the events of the Warsaw ghetto or the camps firsthand, he researched historical records and collected photographs taken by Nazis and other witnesses. This material greatly influenced his paintings, but his work wasn't necessarily a literal depiction. He wrote: "My paintings should not be interpreted as illustrations of specific events. I am using symbolic figures, symbolic colors and symbolic situations."[6]

In addition, Bernbaum was inspired by well-known artworks by other artists to convey his messages. To create the composition of his paintings, Bernbaum first made sketches on bits of paper and then put them together like a collage. His paintings are highly detailed, precise and greatly structured.[7]

Bernbaum dealt with a range of harsh situations that characterized the Jewish experience in the Warsaw ghetto and explored a range of topics, including Nazi violence, the Ghetto's destruction, the unique struggles of Jewish mothers, the story of the famous Jewish pediatrician, Janusz Korczak, and the Uprising.

The Warsaw Ghetto was established in 1940, a small district west of the Vistula River. The Jews were forced to build a wall around the Ghetto, which stood three and a half meters high and eighteen kilometers long, and was topped by glass and barbed wire. Nearly half a million Jews from Warsaw and the surrounding area were pushed into an enclosed neighborhood that constituted only 2.4% of the city. Transports began in spring 1942 from the Warsaw Ghetto to the death camps Majdanek and Auschwitz-Birkenau. In July 1942, when the transports reached their peak, Ghetto residents were sent to the Treblinka death camp. In January 1943, the Germans began the second deportation from the Warsaw Ghetto but this time met with opposition from members of the Jewish Fighting Organization (JFO).

On April 19, at the initiative of the JFO, the Warsaw Ghetto uprising began. Heavy fighting ensued until May 16, resulting in the death of most of its fighters. Prior to the Warsaw Ghetto uprising, there hadn't been any serious efforts at rebellion against the Nazis, anywhere in occupied Europe. This Jewish resistance became a model for other ghetto revolts that followed.[8]

Fig. 1. Israel Bernbaum, **On Both Sides of the Warsaw Ghetto Wall,** 1973, oil on canvas, 40-1/8 x 60-3/8 in.

Fig. 2. The Warsaw Great Synagogue on Tłomackie Street, 1878–1943

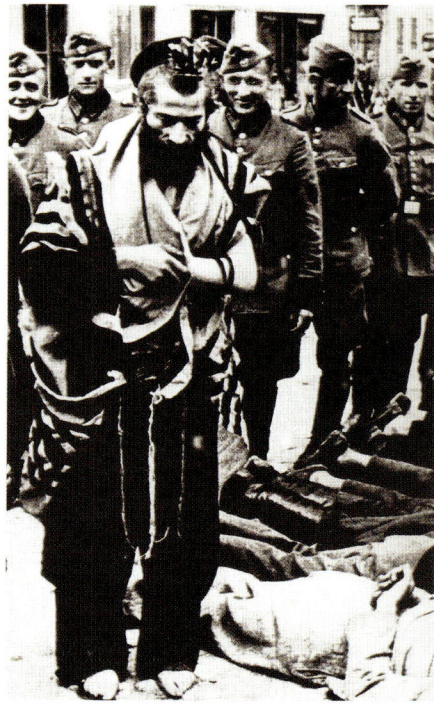

Fig. 3. A scene from the murder of Olkusz Jewish community in Poland ©Yad Vashem

In the 1973 work, *On Both Sides of the Warsaw Ghetto Wall* (Fig. 1), Bernbaum combined two scenes to express one idea as he wrote: *"when the ghetto was burning, people on the other side were having a good time and laughing."* On the left side—the Polish part of Warsaw—he depicts a festive atmosphere, while on the right side he shows the harsh realities of the Warsaw Ghetto. To distinguish between the two parts of Warsaw, the artist used two methods; on the one hand he describes the brick wall of the ghetto dividing the city into two uneven parts. Although the Polish side of the city was actually larger, it looks smaller in the painting, and the ghetto, which was very small in comparison to the city, is shown very large. By doing so, the artist emphasizes the events in the ghetto. *"The wall is open to show what is happening at the same time on both sides,"* as Bernbaum wrote.[9] On the other hand, he used different ground colors to differentiate between the Polish and Jewish sides.[10] In using a composition of two scenes, Bernbaum was influenced by the American artist David Salle, who used opposing scenes in his paintings in order to create another reality with a new meaning.[11]

The right side of the painting is composed of three different descriptions. In the center we see the ruins of the Warsaw Great Synagogue on Tłomackie Street (Fig. 2).[12] In front of it, there is a figure of a Jewish man in prayer. Prayer books are scattered in front of him with the two Jewish lamps (menorahs) that stood in front of the Warsaw Great Synagogue's facade. This figure is copied from a famous photograph showing a Jewish man barefoot with a prayer shawl and tefillin (phylactery). Behind him stand smiling Nazi soldiers and on his left, bodies of murdered Jews (Fig. 3).[13] Bernbaum wrote: *"This is my tribute to this innocent victims of the Holocaust. His prayer symbolizes the unbroken continuity of the Jewish faith."*[14]

On the left, there is a convoy of Jews of all ages, with raised hands and wearing the Yellow Star of David, and in the front we see the famous boy from the Warsaw ghetto. The group of people is trapped between the wall and a long row of Nazi soldiers. On the right, we see one of the ghetto buildings in flames, showing individual Jews on the building balconies: a mother with two children raising her hand and head for help, a man in a prayer shawl with his hands raised crying for mercy, a young girl hanging from a balcony shouting in fear, and other people shot by the soldiers aiming their rifles at them This depiction is based on a photograph from General Juergen Stroop's report to Hitler about the liquidation of The Warsaw Ghetto (Fig. 4).[15] The Nazi force burnt the ghetto, street after street, building after building. Jewish families and individuals jumped from the windows and balconies caught in flames.

Next to the building on the right, Bernbaum shows innocent Jewish people, including children, who have been brutally shot by the Nazis and a mother protecting her baby from their bullets with her own body. The artist emphasizes the victims' haplessness as opposed to the armed Nazis' strength. Bernbaum describes the Nazi soldiers as faceless with helmets and rifles. He wrote: "*I made the German soldiers faceless. Naturally the German soldiers had human faces, but in my painting, I could only see them without human expression. This is how I feel about them*".[16]

On the left side Bernbaum depicts a happy and cheerful atmosphere completely opposite to the ghetto description. In the front row there is a huge clown dressed in a white and red striped hat and garment, holding a bottle of vodka in his hand, and he pokes fun at the Jews with the help of a musician playing the accordion. A white and red striped turning carousel increases the festive mood. Next to the clown, a smiling priest and a little Polish boy are standing and watching the tragic fate of the Jewish people. The priest represents the Polish Catholic Church, which kept silent and did nothing to help the Jewish population, even though its leaders knew about the genocide as it was happening. The little boy, who watches the threatening Nazi soldiers in fear, represents the future Polish generations. Zivia Lubetkin described this situation as following:

The ghetto burned. Days and nights it was on fire, and the fire licked and consumed each house. Streets were burned, house after house. Plumes of smoke billowed, and sparks flew, the sky wore a red terrifying glow. And closely, beyond the wall, life continued as always. People, citizens of the capital, walked, played, frolicked and saw up close the smoke of the flames by day and the fire by night. A carousel spun and children played and spun on it for their innocent enjoyment and village girls that had gone to the capital came here also, nestled in the carousel and thus saw the flames and knew that "the Jews are burning." The wind blew the ashes from the smoky flames on them. Flying sparks sometimes caught a house beyond the wall, but there the fire was extinguished immediately, while here, in the ghetto, no one rushed to save. Everything burned and no one mourned.[17]

Behind the priest and clown, a white-faced smiling group of Poles faces the Jewish misery calmly and passively, especially a mother embracing her child, as opposed to the Jewish mother protecting her child from Nazi brutality on the ghetto side. The white-faced smiling Poles bear a strong resemblance to Belgian artist James Ensor's paintings, especially in the way the figures are gathered together and given mask-like faces. Whether Bernbaum did it intentionally or unconsciously, the imagery of people wearing masks could imply that they're hiding their faces in shame.

Fig. 4. The Warsaw ghetto in flames, ©Yad Vashem

On a high balcony on the top left side, the artist placed three important-looking figures with serious facial expressions and tightly closed mouths. They are looking at the ghetto's harsh scenery passively from above. These figures represent the leaders of the United States (Roosevelt), Great Britain (Churchill), and the Soviet Union (Stalin), who kept silent about the Jewish nation's fate and did nothing to prevent the Nazis from executing the Jewish people.

Nevertheless, Bernbaum did not forget the people he calls human angels,[19] who risked their lives to help the Jews. To represent these "righteous gentiles," he depicted a small-sized couple below the balcony with the world's leaders. They are facing away from their Polish neighbors, the woman is covering her face with her hands in sorrow while the man hugs her to comfort her, and they both are bowing their heads in shame. Bernbaum wrote:

> **I pay tribute to those very few who helped to rescue Jewish lives...The Jewish people will never forget the bravery and humanity of those members of the Polish clergy and the Catholic nuns who saved Jewish lives.**[20]

Fig. 5. Israel Bernbaum, The Warsaw Ghetto Streets 1943, 1979, oil on canvas, 60-3/8 x 90-7/8 in.

The trigger for creating **The Warsaw Ghetto Streets 1943** of 1979 (Fig. 5) was a photograph from the Stroop report showing the ruins and rubble of an area in Warsaw that Bernbaum came across (Fig. 6)[21]. In the front on the ruins, there is a fragment of a street sign with the inscription "Ulica Karmelicka" on it.[22] This sign affected Bernbaum deeply, since Karmelicka Street was the street where his grandparents, many members of his family, and friends had lived. In order to express the destruction of other Warsaw streets, which the Jewish people had occupied for centuries, he created this painting so that these streets' existence and their meaning would not be forgotten. Bernbaum wrote: *"After the war, when I returned to my homeland, Poland, I found my world, in which I had lived and which had been so dear to me, completely in ashes."*[23]

Fig. 6. Ruins of "Ulica Karmelicka", photograph from **The Juergen Stroop Report,** 1943, ©Yad Vashem

Influenced by the photograph from the Stroop report, Bernbaum placed in the painting a building with the street sign "Ulica Gesia."[24] Many yellow Warsaw street signs — mainly in the Jewish section — are scattered in front of the building, reminiscent of their existence in the past. In the background we see the ruins of the Warsaw Great Synagogue from Tłomackie Street. In front of it, the artist shows the burning of books and Torah scrolls, the ruined Holy Ark, and one of the two Jewish lamps that stood in front of the Synagogue next to the ritual articles, while the other one is seen on the right in front of the ghetto wall. A figure covered with a prayer shawl holding the Torah scrolls emerges from the flames of the burning books and scrolls. Bernbaum wrote: *"the Torah, in the hands of the figure, symbolizes the ultimate triumph of human values and human spirit over the evil of racism, prejudice and hatred".*[25]

On the top of both sides of the painting, we see the ghetto walls that together embrace the ruins of Jewish existence in Warsaw. On both walls we see an inscription written in Yiddish: "Gedenk!!" — meaning "remember" — as a last wish of the Jewish people who were murdered by the Nazis. The Nazis are represented by their flag flying proudly on buildings behind the ghetto walls. A scene of the Jewish revolt in the Warsaw ghetto is seen on the lower left corner of the painting, where a relatively large figure of a Jewish fighter tramples a Nazi flag while raising high in one hand a rifle and holding in the other hand a flag of Zion with the Hebrew inscription written in blood: "Am Israel Chai," which means "Long live the Jewish people." The figure is a symbol of the Jewish ghetto fighters' resistance and bravery. Behind the fighter, more young men and women, members of the Jewish underground organization, emerge from underground tunnels holding their weapons, ready to fight the Nazis. The description of the two young women fighters is taken from the original photograph from the Stroop report, which includes mention of three Jewish women JFO fighters in the Warsaw ghetto: Malka Zdrojewicz, Bluma Wyszogrodski, and her sister Rachela, who were captured by the Nazis during the Jewish uprising (Fig. 7).[26] This artwork conveys a message of remembrance of both spiritual and physical resistance.

Fig. 7. Jewish women JFO fighters in Warsaw ghetto, photograph from ***The Juergen Stroop Report,*** *1943, ©Yad Vashem*

Bernbaum dealt with the Jewish mothers' tragedy during the Holocaust in the painting *The Jewish Mother in the Ghetto* of 1980 (Fig. 8). He describes the difficulties Jewish mothers encountered in trying to protect their children, and the helplessness they felt. In Jewish tradition, the ideal model of a Jewish woman as a wife and mother is depicted in the biblical Book of Proverbs (Chapter 31, verses 10–31):"Eshet Chayil" ("woman of valor"). She is described as devoted to her husband and children, as the provider of all needs of the home and the family's livelihood. The woman's traditional role as a mother, caring for the children's needs such as food and shelter and being responsible for her children's safety, was very hard to actualize during the Holocaust, as is seen in Bernbaum's painting.

Bernbaum describes various situations that Jewish mothers faced in order to protect their children from Nazi violence, cruelty, and inhumane actions. The large central figure is a mother in the Warsaw ghetto with the blue Star of David on the white armband embracing her child in an attempt to protect him. Two faceless Nazi soldiers, marked with the swastika on their red armband and helmets, hold rifles in their blood-stained hands and take aim at the mother and child. Bernbaum noted that "this scene is based on an actual photograph (Fig. 9).[27] The only difference is that in the photograph there is one soldier shooting at the mother and child."[28]

In the background behind the central figure we see Nazi soldiers dragging the children from their mothers to throw them into the fire. The mothers are crying in despair, agony, and helplessness. Above this scene, the artist shows a convoy of countless children wearing white clothes to convey their innocence. Their raised

Fig. 8. Israel Bernbaum, ***The Jewish Mother in the Ghetto,*** 1981, oil on canvas, 48-¼ x 70-½ in.

Fig. 9. A German Soldier shooting a Mother and Child, *date and place unknown,* ©*Yad Vashem*

hands are reminiscent of the famous boy from the Warsaw Ghetto and emphasize their helplessness. In the midst of the crowd of children, a huge faceless Nazi soldier is standing with bloodstained hands holding a machine gun. To his right, there is an enormous Nazi helmet with flames bursting to the sky. The flames are red, suggesting that they are mixed with human blood. A large screaming face of a mother tearing her hair in agony and despair emerges from the flames. She represents all Jewish mothers who suffered the loss of their murdered children.

Without a doubt, the artist was influenced by the famous painting *The Scream* by Edvard Munch (1893), almost copying the facial expression of the wide-open screaming mouth and the two hands beside the head.[29] By doing so, the artist attracts the viewer's attention immediately, since this painting is well known, and at the same time he conveys the message of the Jewish mothers' helplessness.

On the left side of the painting we see two different scenes: the first one is of panicked mothers with children in their arms scattering in all directions. They are looking to find a safe hiding place, but they are surrounded by the ghetto wall and cannot escape. The second scene shows the hostile neighbors using binoculars from their windows and balconies to observe life in the Jewish ghetto without helping.

On the left bottom corner of the painting, Bernbaum pays tribute to the Jewish mothers, acknowledging that despite the unbearable living conditions in the ghetto, they did not give up their hope and faith and continued to function according to the ideal model of a Jewish wife and a mother. He depicts a young mother breast-feeding her baby, while her husband is busy preparing weapons and ammunition for the resistance against the Nazis. In the room next to them, a mother is rocking her baby to sleep. In the following space we see a mother with her two children observing the ritual of welcoming and blessing the Sabbath by lighting the Sabbath candles. And in the last alcove there are three mothers with their children crawling to find a safe hiding place. In this painting, Bernbaum draws the viewer's attention to the tragedy of the Jewish mothers during the Holocaust.

In two of his paintings, Bernbaum describes Janusz Korczak, the famous Polish-Jewish pediatrician, educator, and children's author from Warsaw. He is remembered in our consciousness as a devoted educator to his pupils during the Holocaust, especially because of his decision to join them in their horrible destiny.[30]

Fig. 10. Janusz Korczak—1878/9–1942

Korczak's descriptions show his actual portrait — bald, bearded and bespectacled — so that he is immediately and clearly recognized (Fig. 10). Bernbaum relied on photographs of Korczak and added facial expressions according to the message he wanted to convey.

In one of the paintings, *Janusz Korczak Nursing Sick Children* of 1990 (Fig. 11), Bernbaum depicted Korczak in a nursing room at the orphanage performing a medical examination on a sick child. In the meager room, there are other sick children and the nurses wear worried looks on their faces. The atmosphere is tense and sad, however, in contrast with that, Korczak bends over towards the sick child with calmness, great love, and tenderness.

In another painting, *Janus Korczak and His Orphans on the Way to the Death Trains* of 1987 (Fig. 12), Bernbaum portrays the doctor's last walk with his orphans, on Thursday August 5th 1942, when he, his assistants, and approximately two hundred children, were deported

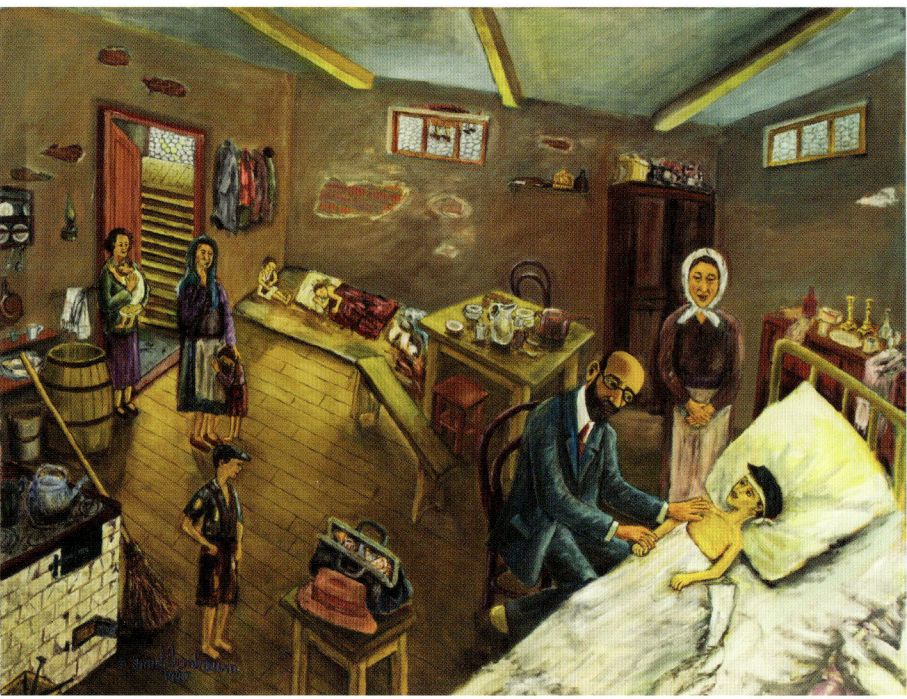

Fig. 11. *Israel Bernbaum, **Janusz Korczak Nursing Sick Children in His Orphanage**, 1990, oil on canvas, 36-½ x 48-9/16 in.*

from the Warsaw Ghetto orphanage to the Umschlagplatz (German for "collection point" or "reloading point"), and ultimately to their death in Treblinka.

Nachoom Remba, the former Warsaw community secretary, was at the Umschlagplatz and witnessed the orphans' three-mile march to the deportation train. He described the scene to the Jewish historian Dr. Emanuel Ringelblum as follows:

This was not a march to the railway cars—this was an organised, wordless protest against the murder. The children marched in rows of four, with Korczak leading them, looking straight ahead, and holding a child's hand on each side. A second column was led by Stefania Wilczynska, the third by Broniatowska, her children carrying blue knapsacks on their backs, and the fourth by Sternfeld, from the boarding school on Twarda Street.

On the other hand, Marc Rudnicki, a 15-year-old boy who followed Korczak's convoy, described the scene differently:

The atmosphere was full of disorder, automated and

apathetic. The children were not marched, there was no singing, no heads lifted in pride. I do not recall if someone held the orphanage flag. There was a terrible exhausting silence. Korczak dragged his legs, suppressed, and mumbled something from time to time…

According to yet another version, the children carried the flag of King Matt the First, mentioned in Korczak's children's novel. Additional descriptions say that Korczak walked at the front of the tragic procession. He carried the youngest child in his arms and held another child's hand. Other testaments mentioned that the children marched through the Ghetto in pride, carrying the orphanage flag. The various versions of Korczak's last journey—both written and verbally conveyed—created the foundation for the legendary story about the fate of Korczak and the children.

In the front of this painting, the figure of Korczak wears a white robe and armband. He holds one small child, while others cling to him. Before him passes a convoy of children and caregivers into the transport car, already packed with kids. One of the children is carrying a flag with a blue Star of David. A Nazi soldier rushes them to get in the car. On the car it says: "Ősterreich Deutche Reichsbahn Wien" (Austrian German Reich Train Vienna). On the right side, another Nazi soldier watches over the scene. In the background, there are two rows of train cars with many children peering out of the doorway and window slits. Between the trains, a line of children and their companions walk towards the cars, while Nazi soldiers with rifles and whips rush them along. Their belongings lie neglected on the platform.

Fig. 12. Israel Bernbaum, ***Janusz Korczak and His Orphans on the Way to the Death Trains,*** *1987, oil on canvas, 48-¾ x 67-⅛ in.*

In one of his paintings, Bernbaum deals with the Jewish uprising in the Warsaw Ghetto, the first and largest revolt against the Nazis (Fig. 13). The Nazi forces intended to begin liquidation of the Warsaw Ghetto on April 19, 1943, the eve of Passover. They were taken by surprise when the Jewish Fighting Organization resisted them and bravely fought back. As Bernbaum wrote:

This painting depicts the courage, the unbelievable heroism, and vitality of the Jewish people who rose up in revolt against their German oppressors. To the amazement of the whole world, the mighty German army had to fight for five weeks to overcome this rebellion, which is known as the Warsaw Ghetto uprising.[31]

A group of five large figures is seen in the center of the painting. Three of them join to hold the flag of Zion, flying on a long pole with the Hebrew inscription "Am Israel Chai," ("Long live the Jewish people") written in blood. The flag and its inscription—

Fig. 13. Israel Bernbaum, ***The Warsaw Ghetto Uprising—Heroism and Resistance,*** *1982, oil on canvas, 62 x 144 in.*

also used in *The Warsaw Ghetto Streets 1943* (Fig. 5)—symbolize the collective courage and valor of the JFO. The bearded figure at the bottom is fighting with a pistol; above him the young woman fighter is throwing a bottle with explosives, and a young boy is supplying her with another bottle. On their right, one fighter is tearing the Nazi flag to pieces, and a shirtless fighter is shooting with a pistol. On the left side of the flag there is a figure covered with a prayer shawl holding Torah scrolls in his right hand, while his left hand is raised toward the sky praying for God's help. Through this visual description, Bernbaum conveys both the active and the spiritual resistance the Jews employed in their fight against the Nazis.

On both sides of the painting we see battle scenes between the Jewish resistance fighters, armed with small weapons, and the Nazis, battling with tanks and airplanes. On the bottom left side, Bernbaum shows men, women and children seeking shelter in an underground bunker. Bernbaum depicted Dr. Emmanuel Ringelblum sitting and writing in the bunker as a tribute to the historian's chronicles of the daily events of the Warsaw Jews, which became the most credible and important source of information on the Warsaw ghetto.

The Jewish Children

Over a million and a half Jewish children were murdered in the Holocaust. The extermination of helpless children struck many, and Yitzhak Katzenelson expressed it powerfully in his poem:

> **The First Ones**
> by Yitzhak Katzenelson
> *First to perish were the children, abandoned orphans,*
> *The world's best, the bleak earth's brightest…*
> *…They were the first taken to die, the first in the wagon.*
> *They were flung into the big wagons like heaps of dung-*
> *And were carried off, killed, exterminated,*
> *Not a trace remained of my precious ones! Woe unto me, woe.* [32]

Fig. 14. Israel Bernbaum, **Jewish Children in Warsaw Ghetto and in Death Camps**, 1981, oil on canvas, 70-3/8 x 82-1/4 in.

Gideon Hausner,[33] in his prosecution speech addressed during the 1961 Eichmann trial in Jerusalem, also referred to the innocent children's death in the Holocaust:

> *… a million and a half Jewish children, whose blood was spilt like water throughout Europe, when they were separated by force from their mothers who tried to hide them, torn to pieces before their parents' eyes, their little heads smashed against the walls.* [34]

In the painting The Jewish Children in Ghettos and Death Camps (Fig. 14), Bernbaum depicts the fate of Jewish children during the Holocaust in many ways. He bordered them with Hitler salutes on the left, right, and center above them and an eagle with a swastika surrounded by flames. On the upper left side children are led to the deportation cars, while many trains enter Auschwitz-Birkenau's famous gate in the center. Children are seen in the death camp on the right side. On the lower right side we see children sitting and lying in the streets, on their own begging for food.

On the lower left side there is a depiction of children smuggling food into the ghetto, either over the wall or through holes in the wall, as expressed in the poem The Little Smuggler by Henryka Lazawart, written in the Warsaw Ghetto in 1941.

The Little Smuggler
by Henryka Lazawart
    translated by Hilda Rusiecka

Past walls, past guards
Through holes, ruins, wires, fences
Impudent, hungry, obstinate
I slip by, I run like a cat
At noon, at night, at dawn
In foul weather, a blizzard, the heat of the sun
A hundred times I risk my life
I risk my childish neck.

Under my arm a sack-cloth bag
On my back a torn rag
My young feet are nimble
In my heart constant fear
But all must be endured
All must be borne
So that you, ladies and gentlemen,
May have your fill of bread tomorrow.

Through walls, through holes, through brick
At night, at dawn, by day
Daring hungry, cunning
I move silently like a shade
if suddenly the of fate
Reaches me at this game
'Twill be the usual trap life sets.

You, mother
Don't wait for me any longer
I won't come back to you
My voice won't reach that far
Dust of the street will cover
The lost child's fate.
Only one grim question
The still face asks-
Mummy, who will bring you bread tomorrow?

We also see an underground scene depicting children learning in hiding. Most of the images are based on Nazi photographs from the Warsaw Ghetto.

In the center, an image of Anne Frank shows her sitting at her desk inside her hiding place, writing her diary. She became famous because of her diary, written in Dutch[35], in which, despite her young age, she describes sensitively, acutely, and maturely, what she, her family, and their friends went through while hiding from the Nazis. By using her image, Bernbaum simultaneously evokes our sympathy and anger at the Nazis' horrific crime of killing over one and a half million Jewish children in the Holocaust. The depiction is based on a photograph of Anne Frank from 1941, which her father took a year before they went into hiding (Fig. 15). Underneath we see a boy and a girl with their arms raised in surrender and a yellow Star of David on their coats. Behind them there is an endless convoy of more children to emphasize the large number that perished in the Holocaust and the great loss of the Jewish nation.

The children's depiction is based on the photograph of the boy from the Warsaw Ghetto from the Stroop report of 1943 (Fig. 16).

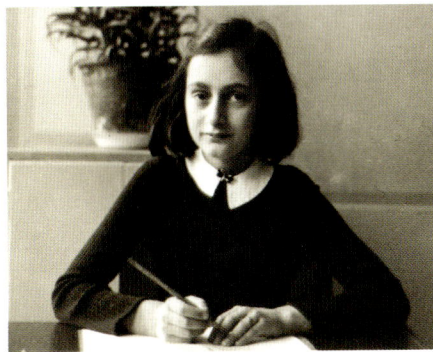

Fig. 15. Anne Frank's photograph from 1941, ©Gettyimages-imagebankisrael

Fig. 16. photograph from **The Juergen Stroop Report**, 1943, ©Yad Vashem

Israel Bernbaum left an important legacy for future generations in the form of his paintings through which one can learn about the Holocaust and keep its eternal memory. In his well-known poem, "**The Vow**" (1944), Russian Israeli poet Avraham Shlonsky asks us to "remember all, to remember—and nothing to forget."

End notes

[1] Israel Bernbaum, *My Brother's Keeper: the Holocaust through the Eyes of an Artist,"* New York: Putnam, 1985, p. 7.

[2] Ibid., p. 13.

[3] Israel Gutman, ed. *Encyclopedia of the Holocaust,* Tel Aviv: Sifriat Poalim, 1990, p. 460. (Hebrew)

[4] Vivian, Thompson Alpert, *A Mission in Art: Recent Holocaust Works in America,* Macon, GA: Mercer University Press, 1988, pp. 7-8.

[5] Ibid., p. 11.

[6] Bernbaum, *My Brother's Keeper: the Holocaust through the Eyes of an Artist*, p. 13.

[7] Thompson, *A Mission in Art: Recent Holocaust Works in America,* p. 14.

[8] More on Warsaw ghetto and the revolt: Marek Edelman, *The Ghetto Fights*, London: Bookmarks, 1994; *Israel Gutman, Resistance: The Warsaw Ghetto Uprising*, Boston: Houghton Mifflin, 1994; Barbara Engelking & Jacek Leociak, *The Warsaw Ghetto: A Guide to the Perished City*, New Haven, CT: Yale University Press, 2009.

[9] Bernbaum, *My Brother's Keeper: the Holocaust through the Eyes of an Artist*, p. 25.

[10] Thompson Alpert, *A Mission in Art: Recent Holocaust Works in America*, pp. 8-9.

[11] David Salle, Edinburgh: The Fruitmarket Gallery, August – September 1987 (Catalogue); *David Salle*, Madrid, September – November 1989 (Catalogue).

[12] The synagogue was built between 1872 and 1878. It was blown up by General Stroop at the end of the Warsaw Ghetto Uprising and became a symbol of the destruction of Warsaw Jewry.

[13] This photograph shows the murder of Żarki Jewish community in Poland. Yitzhak Arad, *Pictorial History of the Holocaust*, Tel Aviv: Yad Vashem, Sifriat Poalim, Yediot Ahronoth, Chemed, 1992, Fig. 87, p. 77. (Hebrew)

[14] Bernbaum, *My Brother's Keeper: the Holocaust through the Eyes of an Artist*, p. 28.

[15] Juergen Stroop, *The Stroop Report: The Jewish Quarter of Warsaw Is No More!* (Translated from German and annotated by Sybil Milton, Introduction by Andrzej Wirth), New York: Pantheon Books, 1979.

[16] Bernbaum, *My Brother's Keeper: the Holocaust through the Eyes of an Artist*, p. 27.

[17] Zivia Lubetkin was one of the leaders and commanders of the Jewish underground in Nazi-occupied Warsaw. She survived the Holocaust and immigrated to Eretz Israel in 1946, and was one of the founders of the Ghetto Fighters Kibbutz. Zivia Lubetkin, *In the Days of Destruction and Revolt, Ghetto Fiters' House,* 1979, p. 140. (Hebrew)

[18] For example see: Anna Swinbourne, *James Ensor*, New York: Museum of Modern Art, 2009; Jacques Janssens, *James Ensor*, New York: Crown Publishers, 1978.

[19] Bernbaum, *My Brother's Keeper: the Holocaust through the Eyes of an Artist*, p. 30.

[20] Ibid., pp. 30-31.

[21] Stroop, The Stroop Report: *The Jewish Quarter of Warsaw Is No More!*

[22] Ulica in Polish means "street."

[23] Bernbaum, *My Brother's Keeper: the Holocaust through the Eyes of an Artist*, pp. 11-12.

[24] Stroop, *The Stroop Report: The Jewish Quarter of Warsaw Is No More!*

[25] Bernbaum, *My Brother's Keeper: the Holocaust through the Eyes of an Artist*, p. 21.

[26] Bluma was shot, Malka and Rachela were sent first to Majdanek and then to Auschwitz. Malka is the only one who survived and emigrated to Israel. Gutman, ed. *Encyclopedia of the Holocaust,* p. 479.

[27] Arad, *Pictorial History of the Holocaust*, Fig. 215, p.196.

[28] Bernbaum, *My Brother's Keeper: the Holocaust through the Eyes of an Artist*, p. 33.

[29] For example see: Josef Paul Hodin, **Edvard Munch**, London: Thames and Hudson, 1972; Thomas M. Messer, **Edvard Munch**, New York: Abrams, 1985.

[30] Janusz Korczak (1878 – 1942), the pen name of Hersz (Henryk) Goldszmit, was born in Warsaw to an assimilated Jewish family. In the years 1898–1904 Korczak studied medicine at the University of Warsaw. In 1908 Korczak joined the Orphans Aid Society and in 1911–1912 he became a director of Dom Sierot, the orphanage of his own design for Jewish children in Warsaw. In 1934 and 1936, Korczak visited Palestine. In 1942 he was sent to Treblinka death camp with his assistants and all the children of the orphanage.

[31] Bernbaum, *My Brother's Keeper: the Holocaust through the Eyes of an Artist*, p. 49.

[32] Yitzhak Katzenelson, The Song of the Murdered Jewish People, translated and annotated by Noah H. Rosenbloom, Ghetto Fighters' House and Hakibbutz Hameuchad Publishing House, 1980, pp. 38-40.

[33] Gideon Hausner was the prosecutor at the Adolf Eichman trial in Jerusalem in 1961.

[34] Gideon Hausner, *Justice in Jerusalem,* New York: Harper and Row publishers, 1966, p. 324.

[35] *Anne Frank: The Diary of a Young Girl*, New York: Doubleday and Company, 1967.

*Israel Bernbaum, detail from **Untitled: Complete study for On Both Sides of the Warsaw Ghetto Wall**, n.d., pencil and graphite on paper, 40-½ x 54 in.*

Israel Bernbaum

Holocaust survivor and artist Israel Bernbaum was born and raised in Warsaw, Poland. His most extensive work is his authorship and visual renditions in the book, *My Brother's Keeper: The Holocaust Through the Eyes of an Artist.* The subject of this exhibition, the murals and the book received the 1990 prize for young people's literature from the West German Republic. Dedicated to the more than one and a half million Jewish children who died during the Holocaust, the book serves as reminder to all children of the world that they are their brothers' keepers.

Dr. Batya Brutin

Dr. Batya Brutin is a researcher of Holocaust monuments and visual arts. She is the director of the Holocaust Studies Program at Beit Berl College, Israel. An art history scholar and author, her publications include, among others, *Living with the Memory: Monuments in Israel Commemorating the Holocaust,* and *The Inheritance: Responses to the Holocaust by Second Generation Israeli Artists.*

Exhibition Plates

The following works were created by Israel Bernbaum

Israel Bernbaum, ***The Warsaw Ghetto Uprising—Heroism and Resistance,*** 1982, oil on canvas, 62 x 144 in.

Remember!!, *1983*
oil on canvas, 20 x 40-¼ in.

Zachor!!, *1983*
oil on canvas, 20 -⅛ x 40-¼ in.

Gedenk!!, *1983*
oil on canvas, 20-1/8 x 40 1/8 in.

On Both Sides Of The Warsaw Ghetto Wall, 1973, oil on canvas 40-1/8 x 60-3/8 in.

Untitled: Complete study for **On Both Sides of the Warsaw Ghetto Wall**, n.d., pencil and graphite on paper, 40-1/2 x 54 in.

Studies for "On Both Sides of the Warsaw Ghetto Wall"

Untitled: Study for **On Both Sides of the Warsaw Ghetto Wall,** n.d pencil on paper,. 11-⅞ x 6-¾ in.

Untitled: Study for **On Both Sides of the Warsaw Ghetto Wall,** n.d. pencil on palette paper, 15-5/16 x 12 in.

Untitled: Study for **On Both Sides of the Warsaw Ghetto Wall,** n.d., pencil on palette paper, 15-7/8 x 12 in.

Untitled: Study for **On Both Sides of the Warsaw Ghetto Wall,** n.d., pencil on palette paper, 15-15/16 x 12 in.

Studies for "On Both Sides of the Warsaw Ghetto Wall"

Untitled: *Study for **On Both Sides of the Warsaw Ghetto Wall**,*
n.d., pencil on paper, 4-13/16 x 11-9/16 in

Untitled: *Study for* **On Both Sides of the Warsaw Ghetto Wall,** *n.d.*
pencil on paper, 11-⅞ x 10-⁵⁄₁₆ in.

The Warsaw Ghetto Streets 1943, *1979, oil on canvas, 60-3/8 x 90-7/8 in.*

The Jewish Mother in the Ghetto, 1981, oil on canvas, 48-¼ x 70-½ in.

Jewish Children in Warsaw Ghetto and in Death Camps, 1982, oil on canvas, 70-3/8 x 81-1/4 in.

No Child Will Ever Suffer in Any Other Holocaust, We Will Be Our Brother's Keeper, 1986, oil on canvas, 38-⅛ × 54-¼ in.

Janusz Korczak and His Orphans on the Way to the Death Trains, 1987, oil on canvas, 48-¾ x 67-⅛ in

Janusz Korczak Nursing Sick Children in His Orphanage, 1990, oil on canvas, 36-½ x 48-9/16 in.

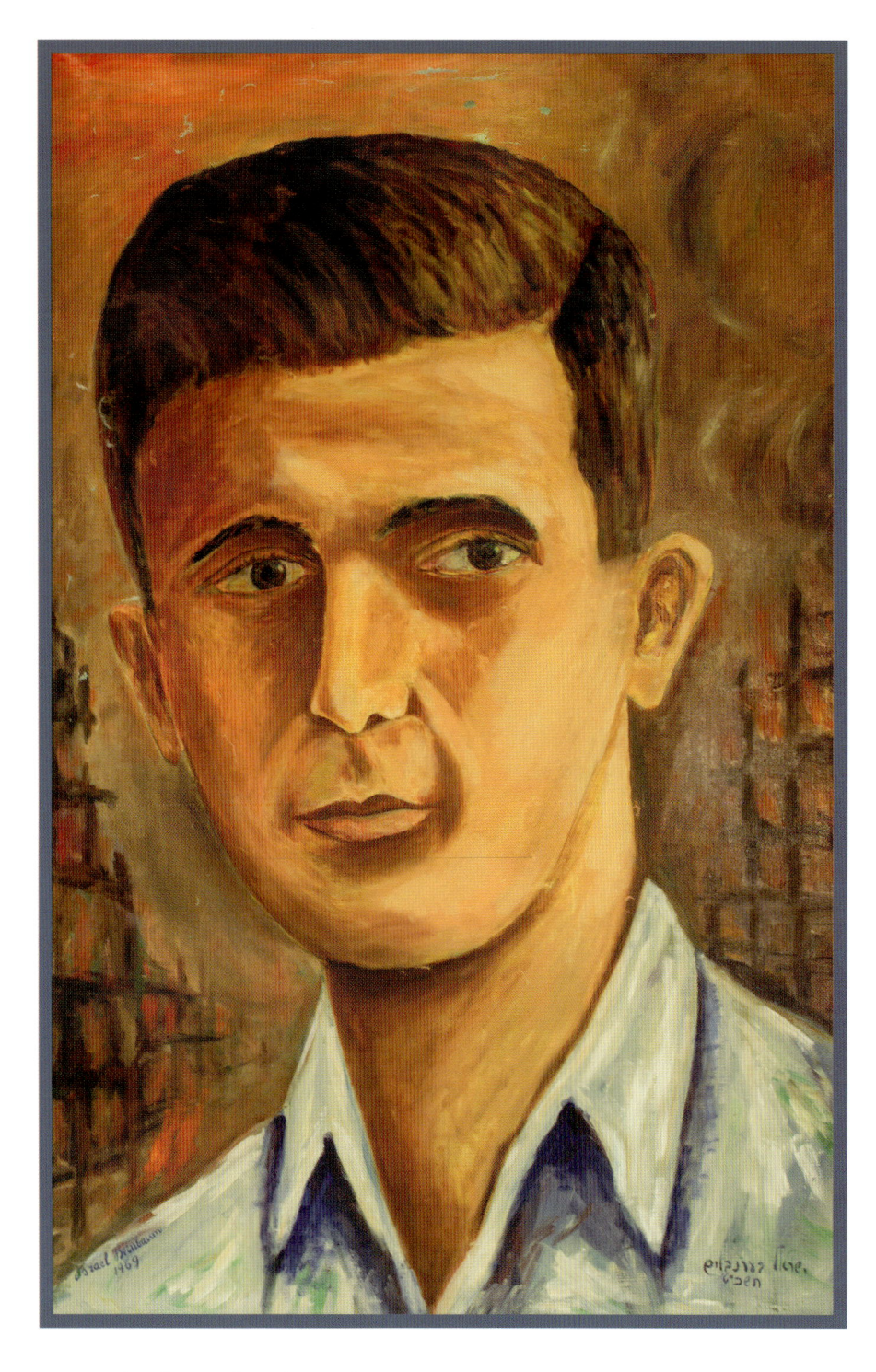

Portrait of Mordecai Anielewicz, *1969, oil on canvas, 60-¾ x 40-⅝ in.*

Portrait of Mordecai Anielewicz, *n.d., india ink and chalk on wood panel, 24-1/16 x 18-1/16 in.*

Remember, 1983, collage, acrylic and charcoal on paper and cardboard, 40-5/8 x 48-7/8 in.

Zachor (Remember), 1983, collage, acrylic and charcoal on paper and cardboard, 40-5/8 x 48-13/16 in.

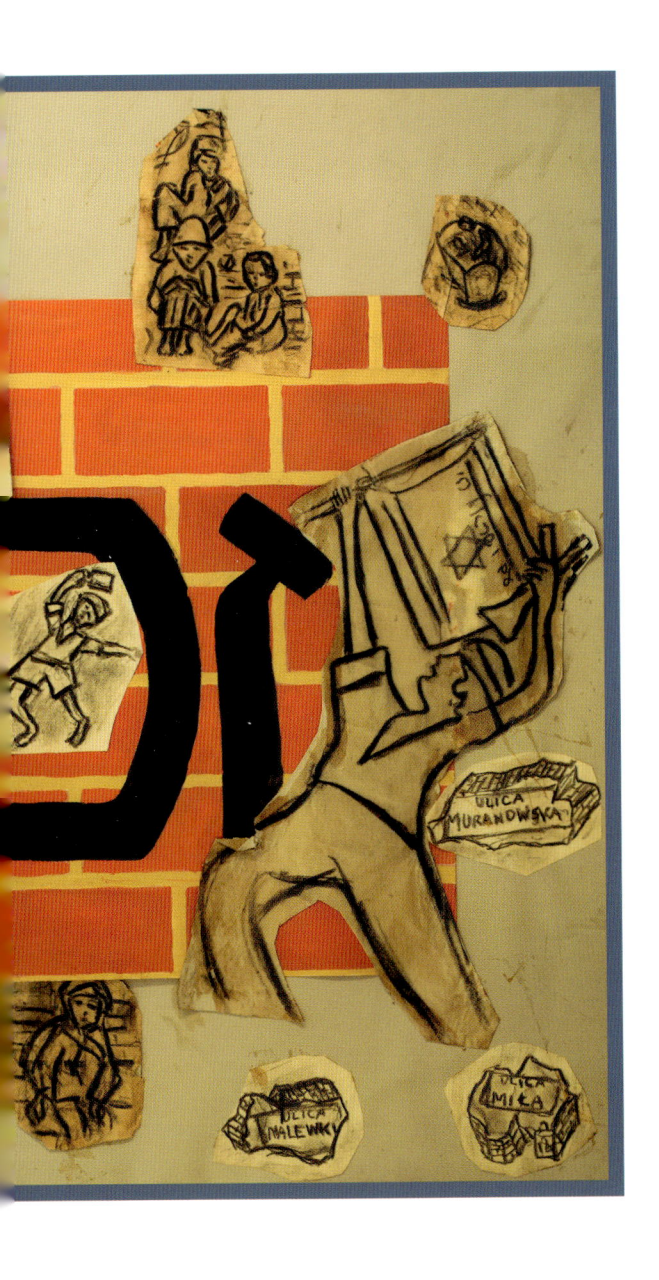

Gedank Six Million, 1983,
collage, acrylic and charcoal on
paper and cardboard,
40-3/8 x 48-3/4 in.

Illustrations from the book "I am A Star: Child of the Holocaust"

Born in Germany, Inge Auerbacher, who from seven to ten years of age spent three years of her life in Czechoslovakia's Terezin concentration camp and survived to speak of the dark world in her book of poems, *"I am A Star: Child of the Holocaust,"* the illustrations of which were rendered by artist, Israel Bernbaum. Of the 15,000 children kept in camp during the Holocaust only about one percent survived.

She writes:

> I stand tall and proud,
> My voice shouts in silence loud:
> I am a real person still,
> No one can break my spirit or will:
> I am a star!
>
> from "*I am a Star*" published by Penguin Putnam, Inc.

Untitled, 1986, graphite on paper

Untitled, 1986, graphite on paper

Illustrations from the book "I am A Star: Child of the Holocaust"

Untitled, 1986, graphite on paper

Untitled, 1986, graphite on paper

Untitled, *1986, graphite on paper*

Untitled, *1986, graphite on paper*

Exhibition Checklist
The following works were created by Israel Bernbaum

The Warsaw Ghetto Uprising—Heroism and Resistance, 1982, oil on canvas, 62 x 144 in.

Remember!!, 1983, oil on canvas, 20 x 40-¼ in.

Zachor!!, 1983, oil on canvas, 20-⅛ x 40-¼ in.

Gedenk!!, 1983, oil on canvas, 20-⅛ x 40-⅛ in.

On Both Sides of the Warsaw Ghetto Wall, 1973, oil on canvas, 40-1/8 x 60-3/8 in.

Studies for *On Both Sides of the Warsaw Ghetto Wall:*

Untitled, Complete study for *On Both Sides of the Warsaw Ghetto Wall,* n.d., graphite on paper, n.d. 40-½ x 54 in.

Untitled: Woman and children, n.d., pencil on paper, 11-⅞ x 6-¾ in.

Untitled: Crowd with hands raised, n.d., pencil on palette paper, 15-15/16 x 12 in.

Untitled: Soldier, n.d., pencil on palette paper, 15-⅞ x 12 in.

Untitled: Soldier and three men with top hats, n.d., pencil on palette paper, 15-15/16 x 12 in.

Untitled: Woman laying on ground embracing child, n.d., pencil on paper, 4 13/16 x 11 9/16 in.

Untitled: Priest and man holding champagne glass, n.d., pencil on paper, 11-⅞ x 10-5/16 in.

The Warsaw Ghetto Streets 1943, 1979, oil on canvas, 60-⅜ x 90-⅞ in

The Jewish Mother in the Ghetto, 1981, oil on canvas, 48-¼ x 70-½ in.

Jewish Children in Warsaw Ghetto and in Death Camps, 1982, oil on canvas, 70-⅜ x 81-¼ in

No Child Will Ever Suffer in Any Other Holocaust, We Will Be Our Brother's Keeper, 1986, oil on canvas, 38-⅛ x 54-¼ in

Janusz Korczak and His Orphans on the Way to the Death Trains, 1987, oil on canvas, 48-¾ x 67-⅛ in

Janusz Korczak Nursing Sick Children in His Orphanage, 1990, oil on canvas, 36-½ x 48-9/16 in.

Portrait of Mordecai Anielewicz, 1969, oil on canvas, 60-¾ x 40-⅝ in.

Portrait of Mordecai Anielewicz, n.d., india ink and chalk on wood panel, 24-1/16 x 18-1/16 in.

Remember, 1983, collage, acrylic and charcoal on paper and cardboard, 40-⅝ x 48-⅞ in.

Zachor (Remember), 1983, collage, acrylic and charcoal on paper and cardboard, 40-⅝ x 48-13/16 in.

Gedank Six Million, 1983, collage, acrylic and charcoal on paper and cardboard, 40-⅜ x 48-¾ in.

Seven photo blow-ups of illustrations from the book, *"I am A Star: Child of the Holocaust."*